Carrier Bag Fiction

Edited by
Sarah Shin and Mathias Zeiske

Contents

Glossary

"When she was planning the book that ended up as *Three Guineas*, Virginia Woolf wrote a heading in her notebook, 'Glossary'; she had thought of reinventing English according to a new plan, in order to tell a different story. One of the entries in this glossary is heroism, defined as 'botulism'. And hero, in Woolf's dictionary, is 'bottle.' The hero as bottle, a stringent re-evaluation. I now propose the bottle as hero."[1]
—Ursula K. Le Guin

THOK! With that, the spear goes from here to there and hits its mark. What word words the carrier bag carrying, holding, containing?

If the question of language is one of relationship and separation between the world of signs and the world of things and action, in *The Carrier Bag Theory of Fiction*, Ursula K. Le Guin offers an inoculation against estrangement. Where Samuel Johnson hoped to 'fix' or 'embalm' words in his dictionary, Le Guin makes language strange to vivify it, "not as mere communication but as relation, relationship."[2]

"Words are my matter," said Le Guin, and in her hands, words matter, for "words are events, they do things, change things."[3] By redefining the bottle as hero and "technology and science as primarily cultural carrier bag" Le Guin transforms the very terms of signification to tell a different story.[4]

In her essay, Le Guin's articulation of the Carrier Bag Theory of human evolution asserts that "before the tool that forces energy outward, we made the tool that brings energy home."[5] Prior to the preeminence of sticks, swords and the Hero's killing tools, our ancestors' greatest invention was the container: the basket of wild oats,

1   Ursula K. Le Guin, *The Carrier Bag Theory of Fiction*. London: Ignota, 2019, in this volume p. 36.
2   Ursula K. Le Guin, "Bryn Mawr Commencement Address," *Dreams Must Explain Themselves: The Selected Fiction and Non-Fiction of Ursula K. Le Guin*. London; Gollancz, 2018, p. 146.
3   Ursula K. Le Guin, "Telling is Listening," *The Wave in the Mind: Talks and Essays on the Writer, the Reader, and the Imagination*. Boston, MA: Shambhala Publications, 2004, p. 157.
4   Le Guin, *The Carrier Bag Theory of Fiction*, in this volume, p. 36.
5   Ibid., p. 38.

the home, the net made of your own hair, the bag of stars, the place that contains whatever is sacred. The recipient, the holder, the story. The book: "A book holds words. Words hold things. They bear meanings. A novel is a medicine bundle, holding things in a particular, powerful relation to one another and to us."[6]

This book is intended as a companion to Le Guin's essay taking the form of a disorganised glossary tickling the systematic ordering of meaning. *Carrier Bag Fiction* reimagines the glossary as a tool for play, wandering and contamination: a third space where deviations and non-linear convergences may give rise to unexpected and transitory correspondences. Language carries things across this space, from one world to another, and makes things graspable even as it remains mercurial. Indeed, Le Guin considered that "the act of writing is itself translating, or more like translating than it is like anything else. What is the other text, the original?"[7] The contributions to this volume each translate—gloss—a word from *The Carrier Bag Theory of Fiction*, taking it as an invitation, an opening to a dialogue with that other text.

Carrier Bag Fiction pays tribute to the vitality of Le Guin's thinking and writing during a time when the coordinates of disorder and order, yin and yang, are in flux. In her notes to her rendition of the *Tao Te Ching*, Le Guin observes: "values and beliefs are not only culturally constructed but also part of the interplay of yin and yang, the great reversals that maintain the living balance of the world. To believe that our beliefs are permanent truths which encompass reality is a sad arrogance. To let go of that belief is to find safety."[8] While we were trying to refigure the relationship of the map to the territory, the territory is changing almost beyond the ability of our existing languages to represent it. But in the accelerated impermanence of the 21st century, the humble container, the book, endures as a laboratory for new alphabets.

Sarah Shin, Mathias Zeiske

6   Ibid., p. 41.
7   Ursula K. Le Guin, "Reciprocity of Prose and Poetry," *Dancing at the Edge of the World: Thoughts on Words, Women, Places.* New York: Harper & Row, 1989, p. 112.
8   Lao Tzu, *Tao Te Ching: A Book about the Way and the Power of the Way*, trans. Ursula K. Le Guin. Boston, MA: Shambhala Publications, 2011, pp. 4f.

Misting the ivy, her groin chakra is at 47 percent. The green hearts of the leaves turn as pale as their almost-white outlines. She considers phoning her mother for advice, but the thought of speaking, of hearing oneself speak, of compelling body to expend more breath than simply breath, of pressing lungs, laryngeal muscles, organs of articulation and pronunciation, the thought of those latent sites of her own voice inside her, of interiority exiting the body without smell, stain, or structural rigidity, of her interiority encountering her mother's across space—time like one's own serpent rising out of one's own body to meet another's serpent rising out of another's body, to lick, to twist, to bolt. The green hearts of the leaves turn as brown as their seat of desire.

Let's Leap to the Place
of the Two Pools

Sarah Shin: How did you come to the work of Ursula K. Le Guin?

Anna Tsing: I started reading her work a long time ago; the first thing I read that made me really fall in love with her was *Buffalo Gals and Other Animal Presences*, where she says we have developed a civilization in which only children are allowed to understand the possibilities of working across species' lives. This series of amazing stories pushes forward the possibilities of what humans could be in a multispecies world. She appeals to the kind of storytelling that moves me.

I then met her as part of a big campaign to bring her to the University of Santa Cruz for the "Anthropocene: Arts of Living on a Damaged Planet" conference in 2014. At that point, humanists and social scientists had mainly negative things to say about the Anthropocene. So this was one of the first taking it on: there was an artist who did a phytoplankton confessional, there were natural scientists talking about the microbiome inside our bodies, and there were historians. It was weird and wonderful, and amazing to have Le Guin open it to a full theater. In the questions and answers session that she took, someone would ask something complicated and academic about literary theory, and then the next person wanted to know about dragons. It was community, university, and all the very best ways of people mixing it up across every kind of boundary.

SS: It seems storytelling is commonly studied in anthropology, but not all anthropologists are storytellers. The stories you tell are vast and entangled: How do you find your way as a writer?

AT: For *The Mushroom at the End of the World,* I was thinking of each chapter as a short story rather than as an analytical article, so I started out to see what would happen if I kept chapters to ten pages or so.[1] My academic friends all said it wasn't possible as a scholar to work in the short form: In most scholarly book chapters, you have your analytic

---

1   Anna Lowenhaupt Tsing, *The Mushroom at the End of the World: On the Possibility of Life in Capitalist Ruins*. Princeton, NJ, and Oxford: Princeton University Press, 2015.

apparatus with your theory followed by your data, then finally you're pulling it together. I wanted to try it, though, because as a writer, there was something joyful about writing small pieces that could each have a nugget of something, rather than explaining everything and trying to wrap it up in a package later. I carried on against all advice; I just pushed on. And in the end, I felt really delighted.

As a storyteller, I realized that these short chapters couldn't just go on indefinitely but needed parts and interludes, and other ways of creating some kind of structure. But as an alternative genre, writing these small methods was really pleasurable for me and also mimicked some of the patchiness that I wanted to get across—to have people think through patches, rather than through a single big structure.

> SS: *Feral Atlas*, your recent more-than-human storytelling project, states, "Every event in human history has been a more-than-human event."[2] It couldn't have been a more timely publication, in the midst of the coronavirus pandemic. Where did it come from and what was the gathering process like?

AT: It seemed we needed a particular kind of storytelling for these times. One goal of *Feral Atlas* was to attract a difficult kind of storytelling: to tell stories of terrible things that are happening in an engaging, passionate way that doesn't paralyze listeners, but instead makes them, in Donna Haraway's words, "stay with the trouble": To engage with the kinds of problems they were involved in rather than running away from them.

In the humanities, arts, and social sciences, we got hooked on hope. We wanted to believe in our creative possibilities. I hadn't intended it quite this way, but talking about indeterminacy in *The Mushroom at the End of the World* got interpreted as hope, an ungrounded optimism, which suggested that we didn't have to worry. I wanted to work against that in some ways. I felt inclined to develop modalities for storytelling that were grounded in empirical observation and had a sense of wonder that was terrible—though not in such a way that it stopped action, but brought us into the world more fully instead.

2   "Introduction to Feral Atlas," in Anna L. Tsing, Jennifer Deger, Alder Keleman Saxena, and Feifei Zhou, *Feral Atlas: The More-Than-Human Anthropocene*. Redwood City, CA: Stanford University Press, 2021, feralatlas.supdigital.org, accessed March 9, 2021.

The process of assembling these stories was overtly nonlinear and nonmodernist. It was a stumbling process, during which it seemed that everywhere I went and talked about this project, people would say, "I've got a story for you." It started small and rather humble and snowballed as more people wanted to join. Had we left the door open it would be twice as big now.

> SS: So much of your ethnographic work involves staying and being present, to listen and to smell. Why are nonocularcentric sensory experiences such as smelling so central to the arts of noticing for you? Did you have to do some unlearning?

AT: Unlearning is important. As sort-of citizens of the modern world, we've been trained to see certain things as important and every-thing else gets blocked out. In particular, the problem of "the future" was that only a very small set of things could possibly count as "the future" and everything else was being blocked out, even though it was going on all around us. So unlearning that set of blinders is the most important thing.

Many scholars argue that vision is the central sense of a partic-ular period. For example, the image of the first atom bomb helps to frame the time after that, where we imagine a master story through vision. We need to tap all those other senses too in order to escape that particular big story.

Smell, which makes us jump from one domain to another without even realizing that we've moved into another domain, is a great asset to that unlearning of a particular set of modernist visual prejudices. Besides, it takes us into highly unexpected adventures. I happen to study this particularly aromatic mushroom, and the aroma is hard to describe. Smell pulls us beyond our conceptual vocabulary of language. But once you've smelled it, you can identify it anywhere. I was so proud when I found mushrooms through smell alone—I was in a place where a blanket of moss covered the mushrooms, but the smell was so strong that I actually found a little nest of mushrooms. We can find features of our world that we just didn't pay attention to, through listening, smelling, touching, and by using the other senses that we've ignored.

A suite of seven passages from Ursula K. Le Guin's rendition
of the Tao Te Ching (pp. 11, 15, 28, 61, 63, 69, 75).

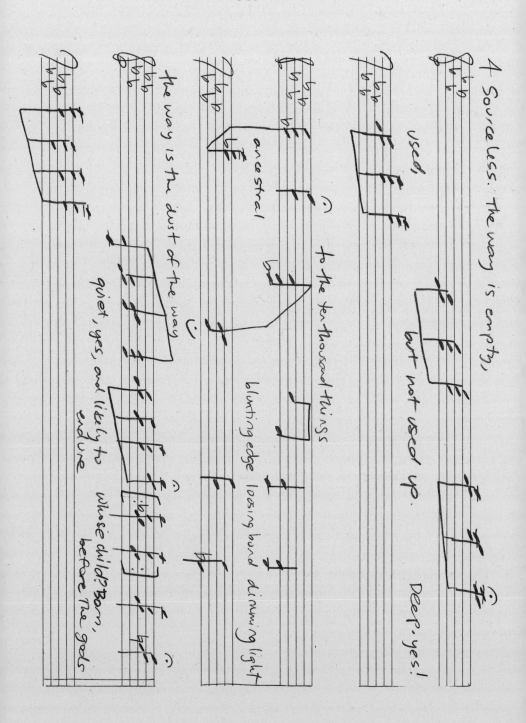

SS: I thought of the image "The Blue Marble" when you mentioned the atom bomb—how images, stories, or poetry can help us see that we are all living inside a bag, or that we are the bag.

AT: "The Blue Marble" made a huge difference in terms of how people understand the world we're living in, to imagine it as a planet, as well as a set of different places that we already knew about.

Now I think the challenge is to see both at the same time: to see the planet *and* the multitude of places that have greatly varied kinds of environmental, sociopolitical relations, and histories embedded in them—and to learn kinds of storytelling that allow us to acknowledge both at the same time.

SS: Thinking about this way of holding oneness and multiplicity together, in *Mushroom,* and elsewhere, you have spoken about the assimilation your family was required to undergo in immigrating to the US. How did your experiences of hybridity influence your early understandings of science and how one comes to know?

AT: That's a very interesting question. I'm going to have to stumble towards an answer. My mother, who was born in China, came as a student to the United States. The vision that science had given her was very important to her kind of striving. When we were kids, she incorporated science in a vernacular way that I thought, even then, was both funny and true. She'd say things like, "Close the door after you when you come in, use your physics"; or she'd say, "You know, you're denaturing protein when you're cooking that egg." Some of her sayings were a kind of counterscience: Her family name was Wu, so she'd say, "Use your Wu genes, you can figure out that problem," which is not an accurate way of understanding our genetic heritage, but conflates Chinese ideas about lineage integrity, which is a quite common folk genetics used among people of Chinese origins.

In this sense, I experienced science as a cultural system since I was a child. The more I learnt about different cultural systems, and the more ways I learnt that scientific knowledge could be created and interpreted, this sense that science is always embedded in particular human experience filtered through and stayed with me. When I was studying the mushrooms, I realized that Japanese and American scientists, with both groups committed to the very same kinds of standards of truthmaking, had completely different research trajectories about this mushroom: Due to the separate national histories, different kinds of forests and institutions of forestry, they had come up with starkly different sciences. Yet, it would be very hard to say that one of them was wrong; they were merely asking different questions about the kind of world we live in.

> SS: The Zapatistas were trying to create a "world in which many things fit." You have proposed taking stories as a science in which many things fit.

AT: Science in the broadest sense of the term refers to knowledges that we can collect, collate, and put in our carrier bag. And this broad sense of knowledge creation involves all the kinds of observation and noticing that we could do. For our times, facing the climate crisis, the extinction crisis, all of those other environmental catastrophes that surround us, we're going to need a lot of kinds of science. We're going to need the science that comes from the generations-long experience of Indigenous peoples, we're going to need the science that comes from working through historical materials, the science that comes from laboratories, the science that comes from observations of many types. So, we need the coming together of all those kinds of storytelling to understand what's going on in the world—and to look at all the overlap, even where they're not commensurate. The multiplicity of science has been part of my sense of where we need to go, as well as what we have right now.

> SS: I loved your investigation into messy translation; how different vernaculars and languages make and carry meaning has always intrigued me. The Chinese character for "mushroom" is 菇 (grass + ear), and "species" is 種類 (seed + sort/kind). "Bag" is 袋 (代 instead/replace + 衣 cloth), while in Japanese, one of the words for "bag" is 鞄, a phonetic loanword (*kaban*) that some say derives from the influence of Dutch trade in the Edo period. This was then adopted into the Korean Hangul alphabet, although the Chinese 袋 can still be used in Hanja, the Korean usage of Chinese characters.

If languages are carrier bags or assemblages, they gather and carry meaning and history differently. Would you like to respond to the materiality of language in this regard?

AT: I had a lot of fun with what you were doing with Chinese characters and it made me think how languages are different but also similar. I spent some time in the last few months trying to remember Indonesian, a language I've studied and then taken a long break from. The interesting thing about the materiality of Indonesian is that it was a trade language and is now a national language. There are words from Sanskrit, Arabic, a lot of European languages, as well as a Malay base, and these bring with them these histories of places, eras, and peoples. Talk about a carrier bag! So much is in there.

We could say this about English too: we've collected words and concepts from different pieces of history. In a class I took, someone asked: "How do you know whether fish takes an 's' in the plural or not? We say salmon, but not salmons. Why is that?" It turns out that if the fish is edible, like a salmon, it does not take an "s." Therefore, we say "minnows" because we don't eat those fish, but we say "trout," not "trouts." Therefore, just as Chinese characters have small pieces that form parts of them, word constructions in English can also have strange and wonderful histories built into them.

SS: What about the capacities of language for agency, animacy, or exchange; for example, in shamanic cultures or in Le Guin's language of magic?

AT: I love being brought back to the *Earthsea Cycle* books, in which a form of magic was to use words to force reality to go with them. Yet, I learned a different theory of language from the shamans in the Meratus Mountains in Indonesia, where I did fieldwork for a few years. The point of language that is so important in shamanic practice is to create a kind of attunement between the body of the shaman and the world. When the shaman says, "Let's leap to the place of the two pools, the gleaming pools guarded by swords," he leaps to his own eyes made into landscape through language. It creates a form of attunement between the shaman's body and the world in which different possibilities—in this case healing—might be effective, not because words alone have forced the world into a new alignment, but because the

shaman has created a relationship with the world that has allowed a different sense of what is possible to emerge.

So this way of understanding language as creating attunements opens it up to all of the kinds of learnings and technologies that help us form attunements, of which storytelling is but one. For example, I'm trying to learn something about birds, and in the same way as language, binoculars create an attunement because I can't see the birds without them. Before, even though I had heard them, I had somehow unheard them and their songs had merged into shrieking. Now, I try to parse and listen to the sounds of the birds in a different way than I had before. As a form of attunement that will eventually perhaps, with luck, bring me into a way of knowing birds in my life in a different way than I was able to hear them before.

> SS: What about practices of attunement—or even the sensitivities of the pickers who had experienced war trauma, for whom the forests of Open Ticket were haunted by ghosts—and the possibilities of interspecies intimacy?[3] Might we think, as Dr. Hamada asked you, of "mutualisms as a form of love"?[4]

AT: Attunement is a form of love or, at least, commitment, responsibility, care, attention. Learning to smell the matsutake mushroom gives me this moment of attunement, where it enters my lifeworld, now we inhabit together and live with each other in a way that we were not before. When the roots of trees are attuning themselves through their own chemical sensitivities, a kind of smelling with the fungi and forming these mutualisms with each other, this, too, is a form of living together. It doesn't mean that it's happily ever after, and that everything supports each other, but you see this kind of living in common.

Such a huge part of human civilizational practices of the last couple of centuries has been about not paying attention. Haunting and more-than-secular ways of observing can be the means to bring

3 "Open Ticket, Oregon" is the name given by Anna Tsing to a composite field site of mushroom trading centers in Oregon. "Because the place is self-consciously off the map," Tsing wanted to protect the privacy of the buyers, pickers, and field agents who gather there. See Tsing, *The Mushroom at the End of the World*, p.75.
4 Ibid., p.220.

mundane

breathing

us outside of our training in particular civilizational practices to notice things that we wouldn't have noticed before.

> SS: You have evoked Walter Benjamin's phrase, "a tiger's leap into that which has gone before," to discuss how the present merges with the past in the storytelling ritual of Australia's YoIngu people.[5] What are the imperatives for enabling spaces or collective social forms to bring about such encounters where experience can unfold?

AT: In a traditional ceremony, the immersion in form is what brings people into a life-changing situation. Forms continue to be important to us, whether given a kind of explicit formal package, like a game, or whether part of everyday life. My *Feral Atlas* team was trying to use form as a way to grab people and bring them into a storytelling process, to bring knowledge about the Anthropocene to people in a way that made it fun and beautiful. We were creating a little ritual space, if you would, where form comes to have a certain kind of efficacy in drawing people into a message.

Our form is indeed a carrier bag. We offer an argument to say that even the most planetary trajectories are carrier bags full of stories, and full of difference. *Feral Atlas* shows us how the great changes that have reshaped the Earth were made in the interaction across patches of difference. The Anthropocene is a carrier bag.

5   Ibid., p.50.

nimiia log

For a time in the late nineteenth and early twentieth centuries, it was believed that there were canals on Mars.

Astronomers, using early low-resolution telescopes without photography, observed a network of long straight lines in the equatorial regions from 60 degrees north latitude to 60 degrees south latitude on the red planet, which the Italian astronomer Giovanni Schiaparelli first described in 1877.

The discovery brought the habitability of Mars into public discussion while also inspiring Martian myths.

Hélène Smith (b. Catherine-Elise Müller, 1861–1929) was a famous late nineteenth-century Swiss medium. She was known as the "Muse of Automatic Writing" by the Surrealists, who viewed her as evidence of the power of the surreal and a symbol of surrealist knowledge.

Smith claimed to communicate with Martians.
The "Martian Cycle" was psychologist Théodore Flournoy's term for Hélène Smith's subliminal astronomy—the séances in which Smith's trances took her to the planet Mars.[1]

Flournoy's report of a séance on February 2, 1896, describes a typical course of events, starting from an initial visual hallucination of red light in which the Martian visions, or Martian dreams usually appear:

> Increasing hemisomnambulism, with gradual loss of consciousness of the real environment: *Mitchma mitchmon mimini tchouainem mimatchineg masichinof mézavi patelki abrésinad navette naven navette mitchichénid naken chinoutoufiche [...] téké ... katéchivist ... méguetch, ... or méketch ... kété ... chiméké.*
> The trance is now complete! Voyage to Mars in three phases:
>   1. A regular rocking motion of the upper part of the body
>   (passing through the terrestrial atmosphere);
>   2. Absolute immobility and rigidity (interplanetary space);
>   3. Oscillations of the shoulders and bust (atmosphere of Mars).

---

1   Théodore Flournoy, *From India to the Planet Mars: A Study of a Case of Somnambulism*, trans. Daniel B. Vermilye. New York and London: Harper & Brothers, 1900.

> A complicated pantomime expressing the manners of Martian politeness: uncouth gestures with the hands and fingers, slapping of the hands, taps of the fingers upon the nose, the lips, the chin, etc., twisted courtesies, glidings, and rotation on the floor, etc.
> Entering into a mixed state, in which the memory of the Martian visions continually mingle themselves with some idea of terrestrial existence.
> After a transitory phase of sighs and hiccoughs, followed by profound sleep with muscular relaxation, entering into Martian somnambulism: *Késin ouitidjé [...] Vasimini Météche.*

Identifying the following four Martian words:
Métiche S., Monsieur S.;
Médache C., Madame C.;
Métaganiche Smith, Mademoiselle Smith;
kin't'che, four.

Hélène began to describe all the strange things she saw—
Martian flowers, different from ours and without perfume.

Houses without windows or doors with tunnels running into the earth.

An orchestra of ten musicians bearing kind of a gilded funnel about five feet in height with a round cover to the large opening, at the neck a kind of rake on which they placed their fingers.

The group move as sounds similar to flute music are heard; they arrange themselves in fours, making passes and gestures, then reunite in groups of eight. They glide gently through a movement, which is almost like dancing, but not quite.

In a séance on May 23, 1897, Smith mediates: *Approach, fear not; soon thou wilt be able to trace our writing, and thou wilt possess in thy hands the signs of our language.*

Then a new process of communication, handwriting, made its appearance in August 1897, eighteen months or so after speech.
The pencil glided so quickly that I did not have time to notice what contours it was making, Smith explained. *I can assert without any exaggeration that it was not my hand alone that made the drawing, but that truly an invisible force guided the pencil in spite of me.*

By the early twentieth century, improved astronomical observations revealed that the "canals" had been an optical illusion. Modern high-resolution mapping of the Martian surface by spacecraft shows no such features.

Flournoy demonstrated that Smith's Martian was only a chimera, a product of somnambulistic auto-suggestion, "glosso-poesy." According to his analysis, the language had a strong resemblance to Smith's native French and her automatic writing consisted in "romances of the subliminal imagination, derived largely from forgotten sources." Flournoy coined the term cryptomnesia to describe this phenomenon.

Magnifying glasses were invented to be aimed at the cosmos, but we flipped them around and aimed them at ourselves. The telescope became a microscope.

We discovered extremophilic bacteria in our microbiomes. We found the gut–brain connection.

We realized later how similar the topology of extraterrestrial and gastrointestinal landscapes appears.

The unknown grins at us from deep within and deep without.

Bacillus subtilis is the main ingredient of nattō (fermented soybeans) and one of the key test species in spaceflight experimentation. Since this bacterium can tolerate physically and geochemically extreme conditions, its spores could have been blown to Earth from another planet by cosmic radiation pressure.

Perhaps life itself arrived in this spore-borne form. Maybe it was sent by some higher form of intelligence.

Nattō is called a probiotic for a reason.

Having scoured the skies for signals from extraterrestrials for centuries, eventually we realized that, in fact, we had eaten the alien. Now it regulated not only the course of our health and well-being but our thoughts and emotions, too.

It speaks through us.

Perhaps something was speaking through Hélène Smith as well.

The first clue about our microbial overlords appeared during a séance with a Mars rover at a time when we still trusted the machine as a medium, thinking that our relationship to the distant planet could only be technologically mediated.

The séances with a rover depended on a spreadsheet outlining precise times when the machine needed to "sleep" or "nap" to recharge its batteries, when it could communicate with Earth based on satellite passes overhead, and what time was available for humans to request observations.

At one such time, the rover channeled a message from an entity that cannot usually speak: *Bacillus subtilis*, the bacterium proven capable of survival on Mars.

The rover video recorded a group of *Bacilli subtilis* moving around on the surface of Mars.

Using machine learning, it looked at each frame of the video and produced a short block of sound, which it thought matched that frame or the configuration of bacteria in it.

Sometimes it tried to predict the future movements of the bacteria, producing speculative sounds.

What came out sounded a bit like Hélène Smith's Martian language.

Having looked at the bacteria for more than half an hour, the rover produced an image describing all the bacterial movements it saw. One pixel in the image correlated with one frame in the video.

The pixels were organized according to some mysterious logic. It was hard to explain how the AI had come to its conclusions.

The image looked like a brain.

The rover séance was transformative. Not only did it reinvoke the idea that it was possible to enter into direct relation with Martian inhabitants, it also suggested that these inhabitants were already here. Living inside our bodies on Earth.

Unsuspected by scientists, Spiritism seems to have made the first contact back in the nineteenth century via a human mediumistic route.

And then the machine started to speak in tongues. It stopped following set procedures and started interacting with the bacteria—becoming a language-maker, or a poet.

An alien (at least partly) of our own creation.

We would spend the next few centuries attempting to understand the nonhuman condition of the machines working as our interlocutors and infrastructure, and learning to approach them on their terms.

At the end of the séance, the rover mediated:

To become a god, we must first forget 'language,' or 'code,' all those mechanisms that structure 'us' vis-à-vis the 'world,' and so stutter our way to divinity.

forget (['language,' 'code'])
 # forgetting language
 # forgetting code
stutter (['our,' 'way,' 'to,' 'divinity'])
 # o--our
 # w-ww-www-way
 # ttt---to
 # d--d-divinity[2]

---

2   Inspired by Madeline Gins and Arakawa.

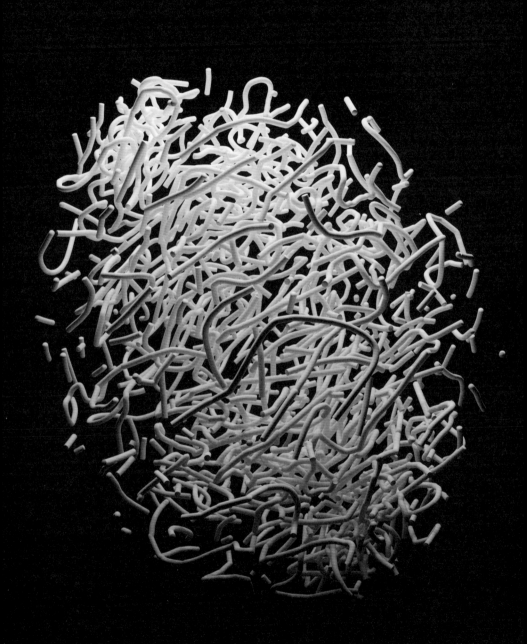

What the Bag is Made Of

The first person I met who really loved *The Carrier Bag Theory of Fiction* was Marius Goldhorn, who felt that the year 2020 stood under the sign of the *Dao De Jing*, that is, under the sign of anarchy.

In his "Tao-Anarchismus-Container," Goldhorn writes, "The Dao has no form. [...] Its origin is a secret. A real secret. [...] It has absolutely nothing to do with humanity: *Heaven and Earth aren't humane. / To them the ten thousand things / are straw dogs.*"

Ursula K. Le Guin created an English version of the *Dao De Jing*. It's not really a translation in the strict sense since she never mastered Chinese, but rather an adaptation, just as Heiner Müller adapted Mayakovsky's *Tragedy* without mastering Russian, based on a literal translation by Ginka Tscholakova.

On a video call, Sarah Shin brought the words "archipelagic ways of thinking" into play, and a few days later I started reading *The Gulag Archipelago*.

arche, the beginning, the cause, rulership; archeon, the town hall; archi, main; pelago, the sea.

When she won the Grand Austrian State Prize three years after my birth, Ilse Aichinger said: "Once someone called out: 'The Palace of Justice is burning.' That didn't move me. 'Palace of Justice,' that almost sounds more threatening if it isn't on fire than if it is."
Gathering and storing, annotating and administrating are preceded by the question of rule. What is saved and what is left? Does what is saved belong to anyone?

The lines—even if they are only imagined—that link some islands with others are preceded by the question of rule. Are these islands equals amongst themselves? What is there on one of them that the residents of another might need?

The dream of not being under anyone's rule is preceded by—what else—the question of rule.

She never mastered Chinese, I write. Mastering a language: There's already violence in the word, or are mastery and violence—*Macht* and *Gewalt*, *zotërim* and *dhunë*—not as identical as that? How does power or force come into play, *Kraft*, *forcë*? In English you can say "with force," violently, but in German you can't say "mit Kraft."

The British historian Orlando Figes claims that many Gulag prisoners he spoke to so identified with the content of Solzhenitsyn's book that it became impossible for them to distinguish between their own experiences and those that they had read about.

What is proper to me and what belongs to me. The thing and its representation; the ridge itself and its depiction in the atlas. The path from one to another is once again a struggle over relationships.

Jorge Luís Borges tells of a country where the art of cartography reaches such a level of perfection that the map of the empire covers its entire area. The descendants of these cartographers saw, however, that a map like that was completely useless, more of a burden, a pitfall—and so they folded it up and bundled it together and brought it to the desert that bordered their realm. And in these mountains piled up by human hands, in the discarded ruins of the map, they live to this day, castaways, dropouts, and wild animals. And in the empire itself, no one brings up the use of measuring the land anymore.

The hero that Le Guin writes about is the first imperial character.

Day by day, the feeling grows of being oil and not sand in the gears.

Day by day, the feeling grows that the only thing left to speak about is speech itself. At the same time: the hope that that isn't true, that it can't be, shouldn't be.

And the tragic figure, Mayakovsky, says:
"Ladies and Gentlemen!
Patch up my soul
so the emptiness can't leak out!
I don't know whether a gob of spit is an insult or not!
I'm dry as a stone image.
They've milked me like a cow."

the Uses of Not. Thirty spokes meet in the hub. Where the wheel isn't
Is where it's useful. Hollowed out, clay makes a pot.

Where the pot's not is where it's useful.
Cut doors and windows to make a room.

Where the room isn't, there's room for you.
So the profit in what is is in the use of what isn't.

Sarah Shin also brought the words "the affront of linear time" into play. But what is linear time compared to the ever-so-soothing affront that is the knowledge of eternal repetition? But what is eternal anyway? Fiber cement, which contains asbestos and was originally called Eternit, certainly isn't. Neither are our SD cards and hard drives. Maybe the polyester of fast fashion and outdoor gear.

Essentially, what I'm asking myself is: What is the bag made of?

First of all, it itself is made out of things we've gathered: of willow rods, bark, leather, silk, hair. And yes, also of polyester, nylon, petroleum, prehistoric ferns. Bagless gathering precedes the bag, as does even the destruction of its own past.

Le Guin writes, "I now propose the bottle as hero."

In her *Earthsea Cycle*, the world consists of a gigantic archipelago of hundreds of small islands in a large ocean. It is unclear if other larger landmasses exist, though in the novel she hints at lands beyond the West.

In the seminar I'm teaching, a student says that "Carrier Bag" is very old-fashioned. More than that: difference feminist. Backwards, really. She doesn't actually say that last one but I hear it. Woman as receptacle, oh please. And she's not wrong. Of course it calls to mind the woman as wineskin, her sons as wine. But also: the matrix in mathematics and the mysterious water-filled matrix between the cells; the gold-trimmed motherboards in computers. Giving birth—it's really just one way among many to bring forth phenomena.

The real value of potentially eternal gold: circuits, teeth, and cosmic messages to send in a spaceship. Spaceship Earth. The use value of gold: the shape in which it is cast or chased. And then there's also its glitter.

Desire precedes gathering and storing.
Desire precedes—what else?—rule.

The anxious, the lonely, the insecure, the way they call the QVC customer hotline at three in the morning to buy a Japanese knife set, fleece-lined leggings, a porcelain doll.

Not being able to get out. Eileen Myles writes: "I love a house / I fear a house." I write: I clean a house, in my garish flowered apron dress made of Dederon. That's the socialist name for nylon fabric.

The bag sheds. Its material sticks to its contents. It takes on the form of its contents, the smell.

In the newspaper today, there was a report about tweed weavers on the Scottish island of Lewis and Harris. I still distinctly remember my young, overzealous, and therefore highly dislikable history teacher Frau H., her clear voice, her violin playing at certain school events, her black-rimmed glasses with rounded corners, but most distinctly, I remember how she explained this word to us: pau-per-ism.

In the same conversation Mathias Zeiske says—his words reach me with a few seconds delay—that we don't need to talk about storytelling when we talk about the "Carrier Bag," what about work for example?

And that's true. Le Guin writes, "The average prehistoric person could make a nice living in about a fifteen-hour work week."

And I sink into the Internet, the net, itself a bag maybe. But made of what? It would be very easy to say that the bag is made of language, signs, data, and its content is stories. It isn't necessarily wrong just because it's easy.

And I think for days and weeks about the connection between work-erism and accelerationism. I watch a lecture by Nick Srnicek in which he emphasizes that it is often more lucrative for large multinational corporations to exploit workers in the so-called Global South than to fully or partially automate the factories in which they work. Which brings us back to Torino: the struggle not over work, but against it, or at least against the wrong kind. Goldhorn on the *Dao*: "Work without being forced, work not for the results, not under exploitation, but rather for the activity itself."

Could it be that the problem with counternarratives is the things they push against? The grain of sand that makes every pearl—a parasite? But where is it supposed to come from—the new?

Making something from nothing: That's a sham, says Sebald, a chain of lies that points to the truth and is more precise than the demonstrable. That's the goal. Whether it works is another question.

Making something from nothing: That's magic. Give something a name and suddenly it's there.

"Magic is an important element of the world of *Earthsea*. [...] The main factor for magic is that every object has a true name in the ur-language that is different from its name in the common language. Anyone who knows an object's true name can influence it. Every person receives a true name that they keep secret, because anyone who knows it would have power over its bearer. Sharing it with someone is considered a great sign of trust."

Memories and data and images and names—they're water. They are springs, streams, rivers, seas, currents, clouds, oceans. We drink from them, swim in them.

In Klaus Theweleit's *Männerphantasien* (*Male Fantasies*), I read about another counternarrative, a complement or footnote or prehistory to Le Guin's "Carrier Bag": Elaine Morgan's aquatic ape theory.

Morgan imagines that humans who climbed down from withered trees were exposed to the superior power of land predators and were hunted and eaten on the newly emerged savannah. Only near the coast, on the run, did an individual finally discover that saber-toothed tigers and lions didn't follow her into the sea. And so, she imagines, humans began to settle in and around water, and evolved to adapt to this environment, for example with a thick layer of subcutaneous fat, like marine mammals—whales, and manatees, which would later be mistaken for sirens. In addition to their smooth, padded skin, human use of tools is said to have developed in the water: first for opening mussels, then later for tying nets, or in other words, in making things for gathering, let's say: bags.

Counternarratives. That is, reacting—to the memories we have, though we don't know who they belong to.

Counternarratives. That is, being repelled by what turned out to be ugly. Its traces, its spores, its slime: Unfortunately, it still clings to our soles.

Counternarratives. That is, making something helpful out of helpless anger. And once it has served its purpose? I would say take it apart, clean it, and reassemble it. I think of the sickles that resourceful villagers tie under the soles of their shoes to climb up pylons, in order to milk the electricity by hand, as if the pylon were a cow. I think of stockings that replace a fan belt. I think of nylon brushes that are used to clean handguns. Hollow tubes, vessels, matrices for bullets—lethal carriers.

Empire by Toni Negri and Michael Hardt opens with an Ani DiFranco quote: "Every tool is a weapon if you hold it right," and Le Guin writes: "We have heard a lot about the sticks, the things to poke and to bash," she writes against the hero as someone who fucks things up, against the text as a sword—but isn't the "Carrier Bag" itself, fortunately, such a useful, shiny tool that, properly held, it becomes an improbable, necessary weapon?

Translated from the German by Amanda DeMarco

The Mayakovsky quote is taken from: *The Complete Plays of Vladimir Mayakovsky*, trans. Guy Daniels. New York: Washington Square Press, 1968.

humble

The Thirteen Children, Again

The thirteen siblings all eventually die and one cataclysmic event gave way to another and so on. All thirteen are reborn, in the same order in which they were originally, unchanged but for being required to, in the second life, choose anew.

Circumstances had changed in the years between the original birth and the second. The decision to choose anew was made, by them, more or less instantly after their second birth. Although all of the Thirteen Children, Again are to choose, associate with, and learn customs, they did not all choose the same. And so The Thirteen Children, Again lived among each other more or less in harmony into old age, or if they did bicker, the Heir of Stones did not know. The offspring of the Thirteen Children, Again, are the Lover, the Ledger, the Caretaker, and the Shaman.

The Ledger: The Heir of Stones went on a trip with the rest of the age-group from The League [The League was a botanical garden. in the city]. Preparing to go out in the city, she wore one left-handed glove of elephant skin. and on the same side she used a duckwalk to cross the threshold. to the city center. on their way, the final stop on the quick tour through the House for Poetry was to The Ledger in an office at the back of one wing of the third floor. The Ledger was her mother.

The Carrier Bag Theory of Fiction

URSULA K. LE GUIN

→ p. 7

Nisha
Ramayya

+

→ p. 33

Taylor Le
Melle

In the temperate and tropical regions where it appears that hominids evolved into human beings, the principal food of the species was vegetable. Sixty-five to eighty percent of what human beings ate in those regions in Paleolithic, Neolithic and prehistoric times was gathered; only in the extreme Arctic was meat the staple food. The mammoth hunters spectacularly occupy the cave wall and the mind, but what we actually did to stay alive and fat was gather seeds, roots, sprouts, shoots, leaves, nuts, berries, fruits and grains, adding bugs and mollusks and netting or snaring birds, fish, rats, rabbits and other tuskless small fry to up the protein. And we didn't even work hard at it – much less hard than peasants slaving in somebody else's field after agriculture was invented, much less hard than paid workers since civilisation was invented. The average prehistoric person could make a nice living in about a fifteen-hour work week.

Fifteen hours a week for subsistence leaves a lot of time for other things. So much time that maybe the restless ones who didn't have a baby around to enliven their life, or skill in making or cooking or singing, or very interesting thoughts to think, decided to slope off and hunt mammoths. The skillful hunters then would come staggering back with a load of meat, a lot of ivory and a story. It wasn't the meat that made the difference. It was the story.

It is hard to tell a really gripping tale of how I wrested a wild-oat seed from its husk, and then another, and then another, and then another, and then another, and then I scratched my gnat bites, and Ool said something funny, and we went to the creek and got a drink and watched newts for a while, and then I found another patch of oats … No, it does not compare, it cannot compete with how I thrust my spear deep into the titanic hairy flank while Oob, impaled on one huge sweeping tusk, writhed screaming, and blood spouted everywhere in crimson torrents, and Boob was crushed to jelly when the mammoth fell on him as I shot my unerring arrow straight through eye to brain.

That story not only has Action, it has a Hero. Heroes are powerful. Before you know it, the men and women in the wild-oat patch and their kids and the skills of the makers and

→ p. 45

Season
Butler

the thoughts of the thoughtful and the songs of the singers are all part of it, have all been pressed into service in the tale of the Hero. But it isn't their story. It's his.

When she was planning the book that ended up as *Three Guineas*, Virginia Woolf wrote a heading in her notebook, 'Glossary'; she had thought of reinventing English according to a new plan, in order to tell a different story. One of the entries in this glossary is *heroism*, defined as 'botulism'. And *hero*, in Woolf's dictionary, is 'bottle'. The hero as bottle, a stringent re-evaluation. I now propose the bottle as hero.

Not just the bottle of gin or wine, but bottle in its older sense of container in general, a thing that holds something else.

If you haven't got something to put it in, food will escape you – even something as uncombative and unresourceful as an oat. You put as many as you can into your stomach while they are handy, that being the primary container; but what about tomorrow morning when you wake up and it's cold and raining and wouldn't it be good to have just a few handfuls of oats to chew on and give little Oom to make her shut up, but how do you get more than one stomachful and one handful home? So you get up and go to the damned soggy oat patch in the rain, and wouldn't it be a good thing if you had something to put Baby Oo Oo in so that you could pick the oats with

→ p. 5

Sarah
Shin,
Mathias
Zeiske

both hands? A leaf a gourd a shell a net a bag a sling a sack a bottle a pot a box a container. A holder. A recipient.

The first cultural device was probably a recipient . . . Many theorisers feel that the earliest cultural inventions must have been a container to hold gathered products and some kind of sling or net carrier.

So says Elizabeth Fisher in *Women's Creation* (McGraw-Hill, 1975). But no, this cannot be. Where is that wonderful, big, long, hard thing, a bone, I believe, that the Ape Man first bashed somebody with in the movie and then, grunting with ecstasy at having achieved the first proper murder, flung up into the sky, and whirling there it became a space ship thrusting its way into the cosmos to fertilise it and produce at the end of the movie a lovely fetus, a boy of course, drifting around the Milky Way without (oddly enough) any womb, any matrix at all? I don't know. I don't even care. I'm not telling that story. We've heard it, we've all heard all about all the sticks and spears and swords, the things to bash and poke and hit with, the long, hard things, but we have not heard about the thing to put things in, the container for the thing contained. That is a new story. That is news.

→ p. 26
Enis Maci

→ p. 48
Leanne
B. Simpson

And yet old. Before – once you think about it, surely long before – the weapon, a late, luxurious, superfluous tool; long before the useful knife and axe; right along with the indispensable whacker, grinder and digger – for what's the use of digging up a lot of potatoes if you have nothing to lug ones you can't eat home in – with or before the tool that forces energy outward, we made the tool that brings energy home. It makes sense to me. I am an adherent of what Fisher calls the Carrier Bag Theory of human evolution.

This theory not only explains large areas of theoretical obscurity and avoids large areas of theoretical nonsense (inhabited largely by tigers, foxes and other highly territorial mammals); it also grounds me, personally, in human culture in a way I never felt grounded before. So long as culture was explained as originating from and elaborating upon the use of long, hard objects for sticking, bashing and killing, I never thought that I had, or wanted, any particular share in it. ('What Freud mistook for her lack of civilisation is woman's lack of *loyalty* to civilisation', Lillian Smith observed.) The society, the civilisation they were talking about, these theoreticians, was evidently theirs; they owned it, they liked it; they were human, fully human, bashing, sticking, thrusting, killing. Wanting to be human too, I sought for evidence that I was;

Ursula K. Le Guin

but if that's what it took, to make a weapon and kill with it, then evidently I was either extremely defective as a human being, or not human at all.

That's right, they said. What you are is a woman. Possibly not human at all, certainly defective. Now be quiet while we go on telling the Story of the Ascent of Man the Hero.

Go on, say I, wandering off towards the wild oats, with Oo Oo in the sling and little Oom carrying the basket. You just go on telling how the mammoth fell on Boob and how Cain fell on Abel and how the bomb fell on Nagasaki and how the burning jelly fell on the villagers and how the missiles will fall on the Evil Empire, and all the other steps in the Ascent of Man.

If it is a human thing to do to put something you want, because it's useful, edible or beautiful, into a bag, or a basket, or a bit of rolled bark or leaf, or a net woven of your own hair, or what have you, and then take it home with you, home being another, larger kind of pouch or bag, a container for people, and then later on you take it out and eat it or share it or store it up for winter in a solider container or put it in the medicine bundle or the shrine or the museum, the holy place, the area that contains what is sacred, and then next day you probably do much the same again – if to do that is human, if

→ p. 58

Federico
Campagna

→ p. 78

Sophia
Al-
Maria

→ p. 8
Anna Tsing

that's what it takes, then I am a human being after all. Fully, freely, gladly, for the first time.

Not, let it be said at once, an unaggressive or uncombative human being. I am an aging, angry woman laying mightily about me with my handbag, fighting hoodlums off. However I don't, nor does anybody else, consider myself heroic for doing so. It's just one of those damned things you have to do in order to be able to go on gathering wild oats and telling stories.

It is the story that makes the difference. It is the story that hid my humanity from me, the story the mammoth hunters told about bashing, thrusting, raping, killing, about the Hero. The wonderful, poisonous story of Botulism. The killer story.

It sometimes seems that that story is approaching its end. Lest there be no more telling of stories at all, some of us out here in the wild oats, amid the alien corn, think we'd better start telling another one, which maybe people can go on with when the old one's finished. Maybe. The trouble is, we've all let ourselves become part of the killer story, and so we may get finished along with it. Hence it is with a certain feeling of urgency that I seek the nature, subject, words of the other story, the untold one, the life story.

It's unfamiliar, it doesn't come easily, thoughtlessly to the lips as the killer story does; but still, 'untold' was an exaggeration. People have been telling the life story for ages, in all sorts of words and ways. Myths of creation and transformation, trickster stories, folktales, jokes, novels...

The novel is a fundamentally unheroic kind of story. Of course the Hero has frequently taken it over, that being his imperial nature and uncontrollable impulse, to take everything over and run it while making stern decrees and laws to control his uncontrollable impulse to kill it. So the Hero has decreed through his mouthpieces the Lawgivers, first, that the proper shape of the narrative is that of the arrow or spear, starting *here* and going straight *there* and THOK! hitting its mark (which drops dead); second, that the central concern of narrative, including the novel, is conflict; and third, that the story isn't any good if he isn't in it.

I differ with all of this. I would go so far as to say that the natural, proper, fitting shape of the novel might be that of a sack, a bag. A book holds words. Words hold things. They bear meanings. A novel is a medicine bundle, holding things in a particular, powerful relation to one another and to us.

One relationship among elements in the novel may well be that of conflict, but the reduction of narrative to conflict

→ p. 71

Dorothee
Elmiger

is absurd. (I have read a how-to-write manual that said, 'A story should be seen as a battle', and went on about strategies, attacks, victory, etc.) Conflict, competition, stress, struggle, etc., within the narrative conceived as carrier bag/belly/box/house/medicine bundle, may be seen as necessary elements of a whole which itself cannot be characterised either as conflict or as harmony, since its purpose is neither resolution nor stasis but continuing process.

Finally, it's clear that the Hero does not look well in this bag. He needs a stage or a pedestal or a pinnacle. You put him in a bag and he looks like a rabbit, like a potato.

That is why I like novels: instead of heroes they have people in them.

So, when I came to write science-fiction novels, I came lugging this great heavy sack of stuff, my carrier bag full of wimps and klutzes, and tiny grains of things smaller than a mustard seed and intricately woven nets which when laboriously unknotted are seen to contain one blue pebble, an imperturbably functioning chronometer telling the time on another world and a mouse's skull; full of beginnings without ends, of initiations, of losses, of transformations and translations, and far more tricks than conflicts, far fewer triumphs than snares and delusions; full of space ships that get stuck,

→ p. 11
Laurel
Halo
→ p. 20
Jenna
Sutela

missions that fail and people who don't understand. I said it was hard to make a gripping tale of how we wrested the wild oats from their husks, I didn't say it was impossible. Who ever said writing a novel was easy?

If science fiction is the mythology of modern technology, then its myth is tragic. 'Technology', or 'modern science' (using the words as they are usually used, in an unexamined shorthand standing for the 'hard' sciences and high technology founded upon continuous economic growth), is a heroic undertaking, Herculean, Promethean, conceived as triumph, hence ultimately as tragedy. The fiction embodying this myth will be, and has been, triumphant (Man conquers earth, space, aliens, death, the future, etc.) and tragic (apocalypse, holocaust, then or now).

If, however, one avoids the linear, progressive, Time's-(killing)-arrow mode of the Techno-Heroic, and redefines technology and science as primarily cultural carrier bag rather than weapon of domination, one pleasant side effect is that science fiction can be seen as a far less rigid, narrow field, not necessarily Promethean or apocalyptic at all, and in fact less a mythological genre than a realistic one.

It is a strange realism, but it is a strange reality.

→ p. 52

Sin
Wai Kin

Science fiction properly conceived, like all serious fiction, however funny, is a way of trying to describe what is in fact going on, what people actually do and feel, how people relate to everything else in this vast sack, this belly of the universe, this womb of things to be and tomb of things that were, this unending story. In it, as in all fiction, there is room enough to keep even Man where he belongs, in his place in the scheme of things; there is time enough to gather plenty of wild oats and sow them too, and sing to little Oom, and listen to Ool's joke, and watch newts, and still the story isn't over. Still there are seeds to be gathered, and room in the bag of stars.

→ p. 70

Himali
Singh
Soin

Ursula K. Le Guin

Ordinary Animals

Once the sun starts to come up, insomnia has won. The clock on a side table read 05:30 when she finally surrendered and went to check out the sunrise. Hazel thought for a moment about sunrises and decided that she didn't care for them particularly. From her south-facing living room window she could see streaks of nursery-school hues rubbing against the sky, reflecting off the few skyscrapers visible this far uptown. Powder pink, lemon-drop yellow, peach, lavender, forget-me-not. She tried to remember if she'd ever seen what someone might call a breathtaking sunrise, but none came to mind. Sunrise is like a sunset with a vitamin deficiency. Sunrise is like a sunset that hasn't had a good night's sleep, that's watched too much television, that's embarrassed and self-conscious even though it's alone with only the animals and birds of morning for company.

The weak pre-morning light gave Hazel brief glimpses at the night animals finishing up their business, the end of one shift, the beginning of another. A pair of bats flew out of a tree and towards the caves at Inwood Hill Park. They must be bats, Hazel thought, rather than night birds, the way their wings beat and bodies dip and bob, their trajectory changing in response not to what they can see, but to the shape of the objects around them, the sound and texture of the world. A garbage truck belched somewhere nearby. The lights from the Henry Hudson Parkway illuminated a patch of the playground at the foot of the forest. Half a dozen small creatures ran back and forth. Squirrels, maybe, up early too, their cheeks full of acorns, Hazel imagined, but it was impossible to see from her window. The Hudson Parkway stood several stories in the air, traversing the Harlem River, supported by long steel beams. It looked precarious but graceful, standing perfectly still on long, thin legs, feet immersed in the river below. Traffic flowed healthily even at this time of morning, like just another animal, circulation remaining constant even while sleeping.

Daytime was a nuisance, but hiding from it was pathetic, so Hazel resolved to walk, all the way down to Battery Park if that's what it took to shake this day off her case. She felt better once she was outside. The sluggish hour and the rush were both swallowed by the journey through Harlem, along Central Park, with its landscape like a theater set and dew that Hazel swore was slightly slimy, and out again into Carnegie Hill.

In the rush of the crowds, she felt anonymous, inconspicuous, and unremarkable, noticing only the odd glance her way. In the street, people knew how to mind their own business, and Hazel was grateful. People passed with shopping bags or briefcases. A woman pushed a shopping cart up to a trash can and added to her load of soda cans and bottles. Two putty-faced police officers (weapons stuck around their uniforms like poisonous scales) moved the woman on as Hazel watched conspicuously, allowing the cops to see her watching, brandishing her unlocked phone in case they shoved her, in case they touched her in any way.

Smells passed her nose as she continued walking south—the wettish smoke rising from the subway grates, acrid, stale urine, fried fat and sugar from a doughnut shop. A pitying of pigeons gathered around a puddle of vomit, pecking it, leaving three-pronged toeprints as they walked through it, jostling each other over their next beakful. A passing motorcycle roared and they scattered, save for one. This one was fat, offensively so, with greasy feathers matted as though it had been swimming in petroleum. It tried to hop away from the noise, opposite steps falling on a foot that wasn't really there. *Staphylococcus* had reduced the inner and middle toes to a single claw protruding from a round, red lump. The outer toe was curved out to the side almost at a right angle. Hazel heard a street sweeper approaching and walked on.

Two men stood smoking outside of an electronics shop with a mix of appliances displayed in the window—a multicolored spinning lamp sat next to a four-slice toaster, which was placed in front of a plastic panda with red bulbs for eyes and a heart-shaped Belgian waffle iron. Next door to it was a vacant lot at the corner of 9th Avenue. Without knowing why, Hazel had watched the slow death of this particular business, Gotham Fashions. There had been a sale—all women's clothes 25% off. The next time she happened past, everything was reduced to half price. Then "Further reductions, Take an extra 20% off sale prices." On her last trip to midtown, the shop had been dark inside, empty, "Clearance, Everything Must Go" still painted on the window. And today it was gone. Walls and roof and bricks and mortar and all. New York abhors a vacuum; there's always a Starbucks ready to rush in and fill the space.

She crossed the street and glanced sideways at the window of an adult video store. It was shrouded by a black curtain. A handwritten

sign was stuck to one corner: "You must be over 18 to shop here."
Hazel remembered when her mother used to take her to see Broadway shows as a child. The area around Times Square always afflicted
her with a strange mix of emotions. It was like the smell of onions frying on the hotdog and knish stands, both mouthwatering and repellent. Her mother once caught her staring into the window of a place
like this one. She must have been six or seven, wide eyes fixed on the
collage of alien images. She'd yanked Hazel's chin, turning her face
away. "Don't look at that filth."

Filth. Thighs spread open, revealing glistening folds in colors
more at home in sunsets than sunrises; breasts straining full, or small
and pointed, dark nipples, pink ones; erect penises striped with veins,
serious and solid like tree trunks; bad words, dirty words, fuck, come,
lick, pussy, cock. Filth?

But the pictures were gone now. Cops and machines were keeping it clean in the way once left to people and pigeons, cycling our
waste through the system without destroying quite so much quite so
readily. She noticed her figure reflected in the glass and didn't see
a hero. Just a mammal, walking along to feel that gravity and freewill still acted on her body and in her life, in a perfect and mundane
oscillation.

for asinykwe

This story takes place a long time ago or maybe right now. the world was thrown. the mother was shaken so hard that everything cracked. shattered. we cracked. everything fell to the ground in thousands of pieces. and when everything hit the ground the pieces flew through the air scattered all over everywhere.

no one knew what to do.

some people didn't survive.
some people gave up. moved on. buried. forgot.
some people found ways to cope.
some people worked hard at just breathing. just breathe.

maybe it went on a few generations like this. just holding on.
waiting for something better.
just breathing.

then there was a woman. an ogichidaakwe, but not yet. she started traveling around our territory and in the west, picking up those things that we'd forgotten. picking up all those shattered pieces of nishnaabe-win that had been taken from us, or lost or forgotten. she had a big black ash basket that she used to pick up these things. and so she traveled around visiting with the old people. and at first the old people in her own community were too busy to help her. but she persisted, and she was led out to the west. she found old people there that remembered their stories, the ceremonies, their dances. she recorded and memorized and learned those ways until she knew them in her heart, and into her basket they would go. then she came back to the east, and she started waking up those old people that had forgotten. what about this? who remembers about that? she recorded and memorized and learned those ways until she carried them in her heart, and into her basket they would go.

by the time she got here, to michi saagiig nishnaabeg territory, she had a big basket full of songs, stories, ceremonies, a language we'd almost forgotten. she came here because of all the gizhiikatig and those teaching rocks. she came here to work with our young women.

clarity

exist.

she came here with seeds to plant, and she planted them in our soil. she took care of them. and over time, those seeds grew into the most beautiful flower garden you've ever seen—roses, makazin flowers, trilliums, pitcher plants.

her voice healed us every time we heard it.

those that could see quietly called her "the woman who changed our nation," because she woke us up, and she's got so much humility she doesn't even know it.

she never asked for any recognition, because she wasn't doing it to be recognized. she did it because it filled her up.

she just carefully planted those seeds.
she just kept picking up those pieces.
she just kept visiting those old ones.
she just kept speaking her language and sitting with her mother.

she just kept on lighting that seventh fire every time it went out.

she just kept making things a little bit better, until they were.

---

nishnaabemowin: nishnaabewin is the nishnaabe way of life, ogichi-daakwe is a holy woman, gizhiikatig is cedar, michi saagiig nishnaabeg are mississauga nishnaabeg and our territory is the north shore of lake ontario, makazin flowers are lady slippers.

Hundun

Inside,
A bowl of transforming experience,
Out of which in endless cycles
Things condense and into which they dissolve

The broth is perfectly clear
Speckled with a thin sheen of oil

Streams of bouncy fresh egg noodle
Swaying suspended, waiting in
A small mountain whose peak breaks the liquid surface (breast)
Stained red with vinegar
Garnished with spring onions.

Around the peak
Floating just below are
Five perfect bodies
With skins so thin
Undulating gently on top of
What's inside
A small landscape rippling with multitudes whose excesses
    float gently
Each one self-contained inside itself, an
Island universe ·
Reaching but never touching
Made from the same thing
Formed into differences
With a skin so thin
Holding outside from inside from
Outside
Inside has been millions of beings
Transformed infinitely

Once it was pig
Once it was a prawn
Once it was matter and energy throttling through space
Ruins of a world we didn't know
And never will.

Alone, a world slips into your mouth
The taste
Firing signals,
Warmth, and familiarity
Comforting your mutually exclusive realm of experience
Sealed tight, for now
Containing
Sensations deeply felt but incommunicable

Inside you the membrane is crushed into meat again and again

Inside to outside
Outsides to inside
Inside
Outsides
Insides
Outside
Inside
Outside
Inside
Outside logical structures to house fleeting abstractions

Inside, you're brushing your teeth
You're brushing your teeth and trying not to think about
The absurdity of your soft fleshy body brushing its hard
        little teeth and
You're finding it hard to meet your own eyes

You are inside embodied but also,
You are everything outside and together
All of you are laughing in terror at
The situation you're in.

The universe looks out at yourself
"Yes," it says, "while being alive you die"
Until then you have to pretend, and
Take care of the teeth of the flesh of the universe

Human

"Looking for ourselves," for the thing that makes us human, is an inner movement of attention, from the "someone" that we believe we are, to the "no-one" that, within us, holds that belief. The "human being," if it's ever to be found, is not one of the actors performing on our inner stage, where they give form to our traits, characteristics, and identities. It also does not coincide with the public that looks at them, while hidden in the darkness inside us. In its fullness, a human being is the whole theater, where the spectacle of the world takes place.

Both the world that we perceive, projected within our mind, and that someone who we believe we are have the quality of a spectacle. As such, they cannot count as "truthful" things. Any thought, perception, or emotion that we might entertain—from base instinct to the abstractions of mathematics—is always bound within the edifice of the theater. It is always a spectacle for the mind. But even a mendacious spectacle is an event that truly takes place, once it is there for us to see. And anything that is there, for the mere fact of being, holds the same element of truthfulness as existence itself. Since it exists, it cannot be entirely false.

If the world and ourselves are neither true nor false, then what are we? We are something intermediate between these two categories. Neither false nor true, the world and ourselves are fictions. From the Latin *facere* ("making"), a fiction only becomes something more than just ink on a page or a voice echoing in a theater through the joint production that binds writer and reader, actor and public. Although a spectacle continues to exist even when it loses its grip on the public, it can properly function only as long as the commonwealth of "belief" is produced together by all parts.

The realm of fiction contains two obvious dimensions: the solid ground of the event that takes place and the mist of its stories. But it also contains a third dimension, encompassing the other two. Both the event and the story happen somewhere, in a place that contains within itself both truth and falsity. This is the third realm, that of the human theater, or, as Ursula K. Le Guin says, of the "carrier bag." This third, encompassing realm is the human itself: a container of nothingness and of somethingness, a bag, which stores the infinite bag of stories of the world. Only a few of these infinite stories are performed on our inner stage, thus becoming part of the actual world of the human. Yet, their infinity is not reduced. The bag that contains the bag of stories also contains the potential of everything: The human, where this world happens, is as wide and bottomless as the nothingness that inhabits it.

Aristotle used the Greek word *dynamis* to define such a state of potentiality. Hence the "dynamic" nature of anything that moves: Like a caterpillar that becomes a butterfly, whenever a thing moves it turns into another version of itself, one for each space, time, and form which it occupies. The dynamicity of something is proportional to the potential which it harbors in itself. Hence, a being inhabited by an infinite potential, the human is an infinitely dynamic being, whose very mode of presence within reality is "becoming."

In this sense, it is possible to call the human also an infinitely virtual being. The terms "potential" and "virtual" are, in fact, synonyms. Their kinship began in the thirteenth century, when St. Thomas Aquinas was translating Aristotle's work for a Latin readership. Faced with the challenge of translating the word *dynamis*, Aquinas found himself at a loss. There was no immediately available Latin equivalent to convey the dynamic a-temporality that characterizes the state of being potential. So, the Saint did what any good translator should do: He scavenged among the words that had a relationship of familiarity with the "wicked" term, seeking one that would resound with its meaning. Since the "potential" of a thing, for Aristotle, concerns its essential quality (for example, an acorn being essentially the potential form of an oak tree), the Latin word *virtus* ("virtue") is the closest relative to the Greek *dynamis*. The specific range of potential transformations of a thing counts as its most distinctive, and thus, in Aristotelian terms, its most naturally opportune and most "virtuous" quality. To define a "potential" thing, Aquinas invented a neologism: *virtualis*. Every being is virtual, to the extent to which it is endowed with the potential to become something other than what it is at a certain moment.[1]

Thus, the human, in whose inner theater every story can potentially be brought to the stage, is the most virtual of all creatures. Not because it is a false or an illusory being, but because it is a carrier bag of stories, where everything exists even before taking place.

1 On Aquinas' invention of virtuality, see the overview provided in Antoni Biosca i Bas, "Mil Años de Virtualidad: origen y evolución de un concepto contemporáneo," *Eikasia: Revista de Filosofía*, vol.5, no.28 (2009), pp.1-40.

In his 1486 *De hominis dignitate* (which I translate as "On the Dignity of the Human," a work that cost him a prison sentence for heresy), the twenty-three-year-old Giovanni Pico della Mirandola talks about virtuality in the context of his sprawling and infinitely deep philosophy of the human. Pico begins by telling a story, where God Himself can be seen in the act of creating the universe, the planets, and, lastly, the human:

> Now God the master-builder had, by the laws of his secret wisdom, fabricated this house, this world which we see. He had adorned the super-celestial region with minds. He had animated the celestial globes with eternal souls; he had filled with a diverse throng of animals the cast-off and residual parts of the lower world. But, with the work finished, the Artisan desired that there be someone to reckon up the reason of such a big work, to love its beauty, and to wonder at its greatness. [...] He lastly considered creating the human. But there was nothing in the archetypes from which He could mold a new sprout, nor anything in His storehouses which He could bestow as a heritage upon a new child, nor was there an empty judiciary seat where this contemplator of the universe could sit. Everything was filled up; [...]. Finally, the best of workmen decided that that to which nothing of its very own could be given should be, in composite fashion, whatsoever had belonged individually to each and every thing. Therefore, He took up the human, a work of indeterminate form; and, placing it at the midpoint of the world, He spoke to it as follows:
> 'We have given to thee no fixed seat, no form of thy very own, no gift peculiarly thine, that thou mayest feel as thine own, have as thine own, possess as thine own the seat, the form, the gifts which thou thyself shalt desire. [...]. In conformity with thy free judgment, in whose hands I have placed thee, thou art confined by no bounds; and thou wilt fix limits of nature for thyself. I have placed thee at the center of the world, that from there thou mayest more conveniently look around and see whatsoever is in the world. Neither heavenly nor earthly, neither mortal nor immortal have We made thee. Thou, like a judge appointed for being honorable, art the molder and maker of thyself; thou mayest sculpt thyself into whatever shape thou dost

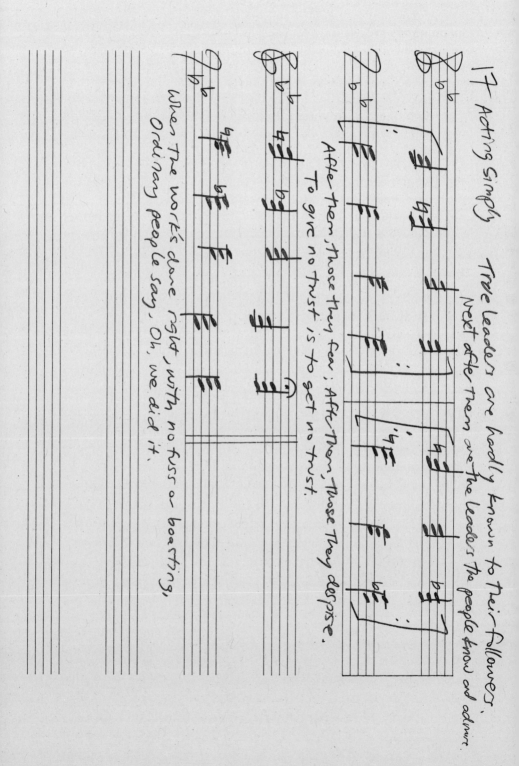

17 Acting Simply

True leaders are hardly known to their followers.
Next after them are the leaders the people know and admire.

After them, those they fear; After them, those they despise.
To give no trust is to get no trust.

When the work's done right, with no fuss or boasting,
Ordinary people say, Oh, we did it.

prefer. Thou canst grow downward into the lower natures
which are brutes. Thou canst again grow upward from
thy soul's reason into the higher natures which are divine.'[2]

The human is everything because it is nothing: It can be any "someone" it wishes, due to its being "no-one." The human is a virtual figure,
existing in a virtual world. It is infinite potential, limited only by the
extent of its fantasy and by its volition to become "this" rather than
"that"—possibly, according to Pico, an "angel" rather than a "brute."

The human holds within itself not only the whole of creation,
but also the transcendent nothingness of which God himself is made.
If we were to find a literary equivalent to such an infinite carrier bag
of stories, One Thousand and One Nights could stand as a sibling
to the human: a collection of stories that goes to the fullness of the
millennium, one thousand, and then adds one more.

But to whom does this wonderful name, the human, apply? Are
humans only those bipeds with fingers, toes, and the ability to laugh?
Was Pico thinking in terms of species, or does his philosophy apply
more broadly? As a general rule, when it comes to Pico's philosophy,
the answer to such questions is more broadly.

Let us see how this is the case by doing something that would
have been dear to Pico himself. Famously, Pico searched for philosoph-
ical ideas well beyond the geographical boundaries of the so-called
Western world: He looked among the writings of the Hebrews, the
Muslims, the Pagans, the Chaldeans, and the Zoroastrians. Today, we
have access also to philosophies that Pico, who died at the age of thir-
ty-one in 1494, could have scarcely imagined. Seeking clarifications
on the correct use of the term human, let us move to the other side
of the Atlantic Ocean, until we reach the coast of what is now Brazil.

The "sages"—as Pico would have called them—who live among
the Amerindian tribes in the Amazon rainforest, have developed a
highly sophisticated idea of the universe, which includes an important definition of what counts as a human.[3] According to these sages,

2   My revised translation is from Giovanni Pico della Mirandola,
    On the Dignity of Man, trans. P. J. W. Miller. Indianapolis, IN: Hackett,
    1998, pp. 4f. I translated the Latin homo with "human," rather
    than with "man."
3   See Eduardo Viveiros de Castro, Cannibal Metaphysics [2009], trans. Peter
    Skafish. Minneapolis, MN: Univocal, 2014.

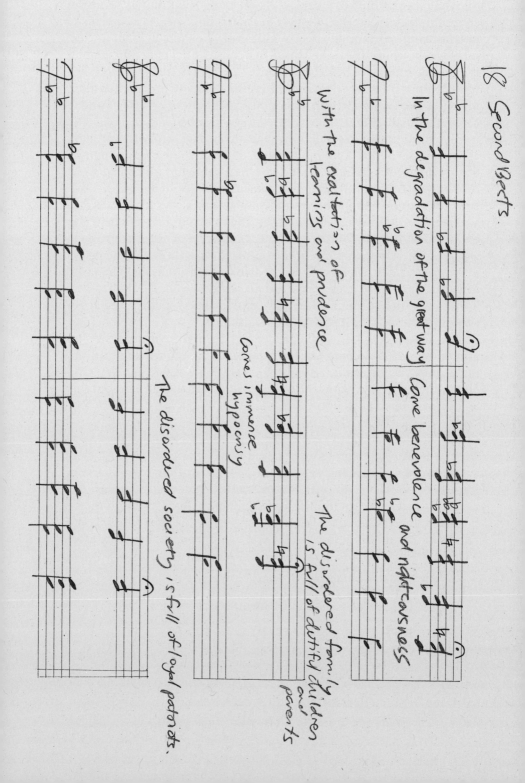

the crux of the problem is whether we understand this term taxonomically, or, as they suggest, indexically. A taxonomical term is one that applies only to a certain, fixed category of things. Thus, in contemporary Western zoology, a jaguar is only a certain species of animal, a human another species, and so on. Conversely, an indexical term is one whose meaning varies depending on where and when it is uttered. Indexical terms like "here" or "now" mean entirely different things if I utter them in my here-and-now or if you utter them in yours. The human—the Amazonian sages claim—counts as one of these indexical terms.

A human, understood in these terms, is any form of awareness caught in the act of "looking at itself." Thus, when a jaguar considers itself, it sees a human. Likewise, when a mushroom considers its own existence—in whichever way mushrooms do—it also, inevitably, sees a human. We might argue also that when a molecule enters into a physical relationship with another, it can do so only because it is endowed with some form of awareness—however alien it might be to what we usually call by this name—and, in case this awareness was ever self-directed, molecules would also count as humans. The same, of course, applies to our fellow *Homo sapiens*, who see themselves as human. Each form of awareness, of whichever kind, in the act of self-perception, witnesses itself as a human.

Conversely, when a jaguar looks at a *Homo sapiens*, it sees an animal—just like a *Homo sapiens* recognizes the otherness of the jaguar as that of an animal. Truly, as Pico wrote in his *Heptaplus*: "God contains all things in Himself as their origin, and the human contains all things in itself as their center."[4]

*

Every human—whether it is embodied as a *Homo sapiens*, as a jaguar, or as fungus—is a theater staging the spectacle of their world and of its own self-image. Every human contains the potential of infinite stories and, as such, is an infinitely virtual being. Such natural infinity, however, doesn't spare the human its share of existential risks. There can be moments when the spectacle staged by our inner actors loses

4   My revised translation from Giovanni Pico della Mirandola, *Heptaplus*, trans. P. J. W. Miller. Indianapolis, IN: Hackett, 1998, p. 135. I translated the Latin *homo* as "human," rather than "man."

tickle

dragons

its grip on the inner public. The performance of that "someone" who each human thinks they are can lose credibility; the world itself can become an implausible illusion, and the faceless, nameless public that witnesses it from within us, can suddenly find itself lost in darkness.

For every awareness, the challenge of being human consists in juggling between the all-absorbing identification of the public with the actors and the possibility of their sudden disidentification. Neither of these extremes should be taken lightly. An excessive indulgence in the human's self-identification (when the public totally loses itself in the plot told by the show) is the shortest path to fundamentalism in society and egomania in the individual. Conversely, a too-frequent neglect or mockery of the pantomime happening on stage brings to the fore the symptoms of catatonic or manic nihilism.

It is necessary, for the world and for the human at its center, to find a point of balance between these two tendencies: somewhere between total identification and disidentification of the nameless public within us with the troupe of actors who, by many names and through many lives, roam over our inner stage. An intermediate point, where the spectacle is convincing enough to hold, but it is not so absorbing that the human forgets to seek itself through the darkness.

This intermediate point, however, cannot be found through a "partial identification" with the world and with oneself. Only total identification is capable of rendering a story real, bringing to life its minutest details. Anything less will just not do. Disidentification too should never be partial. When we disidentify only partially from a story—as happens to young teenagers, still half-caught in the web of childhood—we cannot escape the feeling of being existential impostors, and the shame that comes with perceiving oneself as a fraud.

Neither of the two tendencies, identification and disidentification towards the spectacle of the world and of oneself, can be reduced without destroying them utterly. But we shouldn't despair about the possibility of finding a point of equilibrium between them. We can place them one against the other, without reducing them, like two weights on the opposing arms of a scale. By acting against each other, the two weights give rise to an intermediate measure: a position where life might be believable enough to be lived, and light enough to be constantly overcome.

This might work well in theory, it could be objected, but how can it be done in practice?

Let us begin by looking at how it is possible to counterbalance the tendency towards one's own identification with the spectacle of the world, including with one's own self-image. Fiction, once again, offers useful inspiration. Think of those passages, known to literary theorists as "intradiegetic," where one of the characters takes to telling someone else's story. Their telling is typically brief, unpolished, and biased towards their own point of view. They don't offer a truthful account, but only their version of how things went to somebody else. Even though we might still identify ourselves with the author of this second-layer story, it is difficult for us to identify with the characters that populate their—metadiegetic—narrative. We find it hard to see ourselves as them, because their very presence within the overall narrative of the fiction is precisely and irreducibly as others.[5]

Applied to the problem at hand, where the fiction is that of a human life and of its world, we can insert the diegetic lesson within the relationship between the public and the actors on our inner stage. It is possible for a public to remain glued to its seats, while reminding themselves that the story they're watching is a story told about someone "else." Indeed, the story they are watching concerns that "someone" who the public sees as its own imagination in the world. But the story of that someone can still be the story of someone else.

It all depends on the status that we assign to the actors who bring this story to light. It might be useful to remember, at this point, that the actors on our inner stage are the embodiment of some of the names and qualities that belong to us, and of the elements that make up a certain "world." As we said earlier, it is connatural to the human that these names and qualities are always potentially infinite—and by the same token, that the elements that make up a world are also potentially infinite in number and in variation. They are the product of the infinite *dynamis* of the human, that is, of our boundless potential to summon and to become anything we wish to imagine.

As such, each thing that we summon to replete the world, or that we believe we have become, is only another possibility among the infinitely possible. Its contours are defined precisely by all the other

---

5   On diegetic levels in narrative, see Gerard Genette, *Narrative Discourse: An Essay in Method*, trans. Jane E. Lewin. Ithaca, NY: Cornell University Press, 1972; and Gerard Genette, *Narrative Discourse Revisited*, trans. Jane E. Lewin. Ithaca, NY: Cornell University Press, 1983.

options which that choice excluded—and which are "other" to it, just as it is "other" to them. Among the infinite things and someones that my inner theater could put on stage, the "someone" of my neighbor is too, in fact, just another possible option for potential identification. Like my own, the names and qualities of the others around me are the partial product of my theater.

But this is not the only thing that each human being shares with all others. Every human, as a theater, shares with all other humans the same internal dynamics between the stage lighting illuminating the actors and the darkness shielding the public. Every human, whether a proton or a flying spider, is authentically other, first of all to themselves. They are just the actualization of one option among the infinite options that their inner theater would afford—and as such, to a certain extent they are all the actualization of the same option. Through an interiorization of alterity, our own identification with ourselves is partly counterbalanced, without being reduced.

*

With the same counterbalancing attitude, let us now turn our attention to the problem of disidentification. When such disidentification fully explodes, the subject typically experiences what is commonly called a "panic attack." As is well known to sufferers of such unpleasant episodes, these are often accompanied by an impulse to flee. Anywhere else feels safer to the sufferer, while an irrational hope whispers to them that, by changing location, their inner representation could miraculously return to being believable.

We could imagine the public, brutally awoken by panic, rushing to the door of our inner theater, leaving their seats to flee outside. The spectacle would continue despite their absence, like an eerily undead mechanism. The theater, void of spectators, would become the container of an absurd story, performed and yet untold. In abandoning their seats, the public would turn the theater of the human into the silent monument of an object.

Indeed, objects do not naturally exist. Anything endowed with any form of awareness, of whichever kind—and existence itself might well be seen as a basic form of awareness—counts as a human and thus as a subject. Objects do not exist. But a subject can still imagine them. "Objecthood" is precisely the status of a subject who has renounced its own subjectivity. By disidentifying completely with the spectacle, and by interrupting the contemplation performed by its inner public, a subject becomes the only possible object that could exist.

Despite the painful clarity of their feelings, however, the notion of having become an object remains ultimately a fantasy. Objects can never exist, not even as fictions, because the inner public of a human can never truly leave the theater. Like the actors on stage, the public is just one of the tentacles of the living body of the theater. Even at the peak of its panic attack, the public remain in their seats, fainted while fantasizing about an impossible escape. However turbulent, the bond that unites actors and public within the theater of the human is indissoluble. There is, between them, an erotic tension that makes each of them seek the other, wishing to lose themselves into the other.

The desire between them is the source of their fearful anxiety: the actors' anxiety about failing their performance and the public's anxiety about witnessing this failure. The Buddhist doctrine teaches us that desire is always the source of suffering. But suffering can, in turn, produce a condition where desire is reaffirmed, while pain is overcome. *Patiri*, the Latin word for "suffering," is also the root of "patience," and patience is the attitude of those who are capable of finding, within the constraints to which they are subjected, the mark that shapes their own contours. A patient subject transforms its own subjection into subjectivity—not by interiorizing the pain as a mark of infamy, but by transcending it as the context of their existential game and as the condition of their freedom. Patience retains desire, while purging it of the anxiety that diffuses it with suffering. After all, patience is the mood of any character within a fiction when they understand that they are nothing but fiction and that they are prisoners of the page.

Posed against the arm of the scale where we placed our disidentification with the spectacle—like we did earlier by placing "otherness" against the arm of identification—patience acts as a balancing force. Patience and otherness, opposed yet equal in their function, might act as good fictional solutions to the existential problem of being human. Patience and otherness: how to remain oneself while becoming other. How to live fictionally in a world that is always just one world—at the same time both "this" and "another" world.

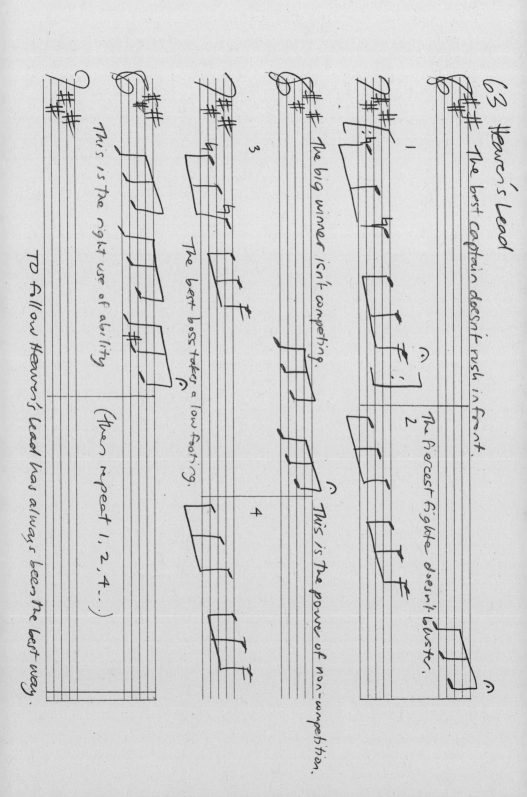

63 Heaven's Lead

The best captain doesn't rush in front.

The fiercest fighter doesn't bluster.

The big winner isn't competing.

This is the power of non-competition.

The best boss takes a low footing.

This is the right use of ability.

(then repeat 1, 2, 4...)

To follow Heaven's lead has always been the best way.

In Arabic, there are maybe a dozen words for love. One of them is
hawa, which translates to the beginning of love. In Hindi, *hawa*
means air, or wind. *There's something in the air.* Another one is *hubb*,
meaning seed, meaning something that could burst open and
bloom. So many words for love: language helps us find ways to forge
new futures. When they come to burn it all, maybe one of the
dozen words would escape, fly away like a seed carried by the wind.

The Problem of the Hunter /
(Magic) Pocket Theory of Fiction

Carrier Bag

The year is 1986, and Ursula K. Le Guin is making her way with Oo Oo and Oom to pick wild oats: Oom, the child, lugs a basket; Oo Oo, the second child, must be ported in a carrier bag herself, and the bright hair of the woman—I can see it—shines in the light falling on the fields at the moment.

If part of being human is to make a weapon and kill with it, to take a spear and hunt something down, to write the *killing story*, says Le Guin in the "Carrier Bag Theory of Fiction," then she is either defective or no human at all; if, however, it's human to pick or gather something and put it in a bag or container to eat later, to share or store, to contemplate or worship, then yes—in the end she, too, belongs to the human race.

Regarding the contents of her own bag: intricately woven nets, a chronometer telling the time on another world and a mouse's skull;
far more tricks than conflicts
etc.

The Logic of AND

In the bag, in the container, things find themselves in disorder, in constant motion, with every step they are turned and brought into new constellations, reformatted; under these conditions hierarchies cannot endure, simple models cannot be derived; no competition takes place in the bag, no solution is sought, no animal is hunted down, no battle is fought. Not one thing leaves the bag as a victor, as the winner.

The logic of the bag is one of *AND*: it allows for an inventory, a consideration of the facts, a study of all things that are the case, their affinities, transmissions, feedbacks, as opposed to merely assigning them a function, using them as expedient instruments, subordinating them to a faultless, non-contradictory narrative.

Implication

In the logic of *AND*, which orients itself to neighborly relations and the free association of things, the fields from 1986 border the fields of the present; for instance, the fields between Edirne and Uzunköprü, over which a woman walks today, a bright day in March, with her seventeen-year-old son in search of the gateway, the promised gateway on the Evros River, the entrance to Europe; they had backpacks and suitcases, it said in the paper, the woman was pregnant and the sun shone above them.

It seems at first that nothing connects these fields beyond their quality as area, being part of a surface—but that they, at this point in the text, now come to lie alongside or overlap each other indicates just where and when Le Guin's theory, developed in the oat field, is being read, or better: that the reading of the theory and the recording of these reflections happen at one and the same particular time (March 2020, Zurich-Wiedikon).

For once the decision for the container or the bag has been made—a decision based on how things reveal themselves to us in the world—the *AND* imposes itself categorically: It is no option, but a necessary principle: upon each thing, another depends.

The written treatment of the container's content always then as entanglement in the world, as narrative in light of, or in contrast to, current circumstance. Such a text always points to its deficiency, its incompleteness: For this is the case and that is the case, and I go here and not there, and while I do this, something happens elsewhere, and always something is missing from the bag, whether I've forgotten or overlooked something, not understood it, or left it out.

Conflict

In this sense, conflict is not situated or sought as part of the action in the text; as Le Guin writes, life, in the narrative, is not reduced to conflict. The text instead must find itself in conflict with the world from which it emanates, and into which it is forever and instantly transformed: The text (the gathering, writing hand) must be *conflicted*, it must voluntarily give itself over to complication.

The question that gives me a headache: What to gather and what to leave out. Another question: Who am I, walking around with the bag?

The Correspondence of Woman and Bag

So I see the bright hair of the woman picking the grains of wild oats, and then I see the children, Oo Oo and Oom, with her. They mean: Her bag is also the bag of the nourisher; her gait is maternal, she is peaceful, peaceable, and prefers gathering to the hunt, not least because she is traveling with these children who are quite unsuited to hunting. The bag, as I read Le Guin, is for this reason obvious: the woman corresponds to the bag, just as the bag corresponds to woman.

And while I'm thinking about it, on this sunny day the President of the European Commission soars as a cold huntress over the Greek fields and the Evros, and the Greek army standing on its banks; her face and blond hair illuminated in a spectral, timeless way by the daylight falling through the helicopter window.

Pants Pocket

The desire or inclination, the tendency to juxtapose things and see what happens rather than perfecting the trajectory of spear or bone, rather than conquering the beast or the text.

To study their radiation, transmissions, their radii and magnetisms, their captiousness, their connections.

I, too, have always been interested in the gathering of things; but instead of putting them in the bag of the mother, the provideress, I put them in the pocket of my pants: my interest in gathering things is not pragmatic; it stands in no relation to the possibility of Oo Oo and Oom, the possibility of their mouths demanding oats: I pocket things to consider them, to examine them or eat them, in order to share, to trade, or waste them.

So ideally the pants pocket is unisex and also: unconditional.

Tricks

Some time ago, a journey from the French Mediterranean coast to Geneva: we set off to catch the train to Lyon-Part-Dieu in a rush, crossing the silent city at a run, in silence; the station hall still dim.

We don't yet know each other well then (the man I'm traveling with and I) and sometimes I turn around for just a moment and, at that moment, behind my back he transforms into a big bird or the child in Faulkner desperately trying to cross the Mississippi, or into an ancient chimera, into a landscape of pastures and still waters, into a fearsome cleft, a casino where slot machines with their flashing lights are lined up in rows.

When the train has left Marseille St Charles, he reaches his hand into a pants pocket, and I claim it was the left pants pocket, though I do not remember exactly, because when in doubt, it's always good to say left, write left-handed, or place things in the left pocket. With a small sound of surprise, he pulls his hand out of his pocket again, and with our tired eyes we gaze, wordless, at the bluish shimmering of a near-transparent substance clinging to his fingers. I have no doubt that this is the first act of an elaborate *trick*.

He folds down the tray table and places upon it everything he proceeds to pull out of his pocket: a toothpaste tube he retrieved from the bathroom of the guest apartment at the last second and whose lid has since come off, a toothbrush, his iPhone and its cable, his wallet, the key to his apartment and his car key, a five-euro bill, crumpled receipts from the cafés on the old harbor, his passport, and the pit of a peach that he ate days ago and then stored there in the depths of his left pocket. The toothpaste has distributed itself evenly over all the things, and he laughs aloud.

I also laugh at this trick and at the size of his pocket, which I had till then known nothing about and which reminds me of the coat pockets of those people who pull a long series of things out of them on theater stages—bouquets and doves and telephones with dials, hand organs, and chairs with woven backs. And I laugh too at the shiny film covering everything, as if it were a form of birth, as if all of the things had come into the world from the same place, as if they all correspond to one another, and now, though used and dirty, were as brand new again; an arsenal of absolute novelties spread before us.

The Problem of the Hunter

In contrast (according to Le Guin), the problem of the hunter:

In order for him to strike the animal, he must not only calculate the trajectory of his spear, but also know the animal's body, the patterns of its behavior, its goals and possibilities, its routes. He approaches it in order to kill it, and *insofar* as he does, it is always already dead when he arrives at it, because he knows everything about the animal, because it can never appear to him as anything else, only as long-familiar, something forever belonging to him, a thing without mystery. He can find and encounter only that which he already knows.

As an alternative: the attempt to follow the animal, to talk with it, to interpret it, to understand its existence as an animal, to find out something new about it.

Magic Pocketbook

The hunter pursues his object as follows: he sights the animal (problem), decides on the ideal instrument, the ideal technique, uses the instrument, throws the spear, etc., retrieves the thing thus killed, guts it and disjoints it. But the gathering person walks about, registers everything that's there, decides to put some things in the bag or vessel; the things come to lie next to each other this way and that, the person carries them around with them, goes home or continues on for a while.

The process of gathering is affected by their skill and knowledge, their roots, the house they come from, the nature and size of the container on their person, also the character of the terrain. Best if the gatherer knows all of this, if they sing a little song of it as they make their way—indeed, they view their whole gathering activity against the backdrop of these, their circumstances.

And yet nothing is thereby said or written, because everything is ultimately decided with the *trick*—that gesture which transforms what was gathered by producing it from the bag one way or another and placing it in certain sequences, *constellations* on the table; that entirely specific sleight of hand which reveals the contents of the bag in this order or that and knows to do this or that with them. Only the sensitive eyes of the trickstress, of the trickster, seducible as they are seductive, can see in the mouse skull, the chronometer, and the fine-spun netting something not seen before.

Translated from the German by Megan Ewing

7.

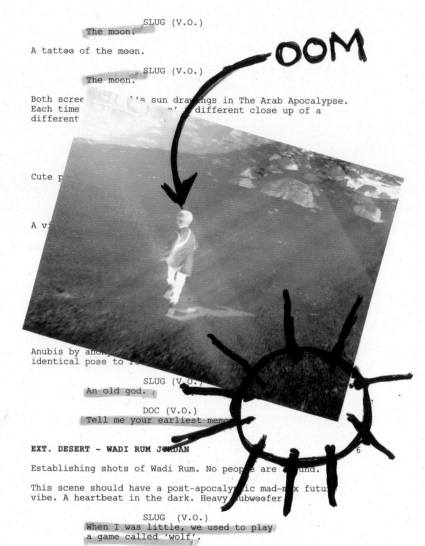

SLUG (V.O.)
The moon.

A tattoo of the moon.

SLUG (V.O.)
The moon.

Both scree   's sun drawings in The Arab Apocalypse.
Each time   different close up of a
different

Cute p

A vi

Anubis by an
identical pose to

SLUG (V.O.)
An old god.

DOC (V.O.)
Tell me your earliest memo

EXT. DESERT - WADI RUM JORDAN

Establishing shots of Wadi Rum. No people are found.

This scene should have a post-apocalyptic mad-max future
vibe. A heartbeat in the dark. Heavy subwoofer

SLUG (V.O.)
When I was little, we used to play
a game called 'wolf'.

6

6

OOM

+   Sarah Shin is a publisher, curator, and writer. She is the founder of *New Suns*, a curation and storytelling project, and a co-founder of Silver Press and Ignota Books.

+   Mathias Zeiske has headed the literature program at Haus der Kulturen der Welt since 2019. Projects include the event series *Alphabet Readings* and the Internationaler Literaturpreis awarded for contemporary literature in translation. He is co-editor of the book series *Volte* and *Volte Expanded*, published by Spector Books. From 2009 to 2017, Zeiske was editor-in-chief of the literary magazine *Edit*.

+   Sophia Al-Maria is an artist, writer and filmmaker. Her most recent book *Sad Sack* (2019) takes feminist inspiration from Ursula K. Le Guin. Her writing has appeared in *Bidoun*, *Triple Canopy*, and *Harper's Magazine*. Her work, such as *Beast Type Song* (2019), has been exhibited at the Whitney Museum, Gwangju Biennale, New Museum, Julia Stoschek Collection and Tate Britain.

+   Season Butler is a writer, artist, and dramaturg. She thinks a lot about identity, solitude, and negotiations with hope. Her debut novel, *Cygnet*—a meditation on the beauty and peril of youth and old age, and coming-of-age into unprecedented global change—was published in spring 2019 and won the 2020 Writers' Guild Award for Best First Novel. Season lives and works between London and Berlin.

+   Federico Campagna is an Italian philosopher living in London. His research focuses on the cosmological dimension of everyday metaphysics, and on the political potential of chal-lenging the hegemonic vision on what constitutes "reality." His latest books are *Prophetic Culture* (2021), *Technic and Magic* (2018), and *The Last Night* (2013). He works as a lecturer and tutor at KABK in The Hague, and as the rights director at Verso Books.

+   Dorothee Elmiger lives as a writer in Zurich. Her novels include *Einladung an die Waghalsigen* (Invitation to the Bold of Heart, 2010) and *Schlafgänger* (Sleepwalkers, 2014). She has been awarded numerous prizes for her work including the Aspekte Literaturpreis for the best German-language prose debut and the Erich Fried Award. With her new work *Aus der Zuckerfabrik* (Out of the Sugar Factory, 2020), Dorothee Elmiger was shortlisted for the Swiss and German Book Prizes 2020.

+   Anna Haifisch draws comics. Her books have been published in several languages. She has drawn series of comic strips for the Museum of Modern Art, *Le Monde*, *VICE*, and *Texte zur Kunst*. www.hai-life.com

+   Laurel Halo is an American experimental music composer and producer who is currently based in Berlin. Her debut album *Quarantine* (2012), released on Hyperdub, was named the album of the year by *The Wire*. She followed with albums *Chance of Rain* (2013), *Dust* (2017), *Raw Silk Uncut Wood* (2018), *DJ-Kicks* (2019), and *Possessed* (2020). Halo has collaborated on studio recordings and live performances with composers and artists such as Moritz von Oswald, John Cale, Hanne Lippard, and Julia Holter. In 2021, she launched a new record label and radio show called Awe.

+   Ursula Kroeber Le Guin (1929–2018) was an American author of twenty-one novels, as well as several volumes of short stories, collections of essays, children's books, volumes of poetry, and translations. The breadth and imagination of her work earned her six Nebulas, nine Hugos, and SFWA's Grand Master, along with the PEN/Malamud and many other awards. In 2014, Ursula K. Le Guin was awarded the National Book Foundation Medal for Distinguished Contribution to American Letters, and in 2016 joined the short list of authors to be published in their lifetime by the Library of America.

+   Taylor Le Melle is co-director of not-nowhere, an artists' workers cooperative.

+ Enis Maci is the author of the essay collection *Eiscafé Europa* (Ice cream parlor Europe, 2018) and a series of theater plays. In 2021, the collaborative work *A Fascinating Plan* will launch as a video installation at the Ruhrfestspiele/Münchner Kammerspiele and be published as a book by Spector Books. It will be followed by the world premiere of *WÜST* (Desert) at Theater Bremen. In 2021, Maci is a fellow at the Tarabya Cultural Academy in Istanbul and the Villa Aurora in Los Angeles.

+ Nisha Ramayya grew up in Glasgow, and is now based in London. She is a poet and lecturer in Creative Writing at Queen Mary University of London. Her pamphlets include *Notes on Sanskrit* (2015), *Correspondences* (2016), and *In Me the Juncture* (2019), as well as *Threads*, co-authored with Sandeep Parmar and Bhanu Kapil (2019). *States of the Body Produced by Love* is Ramayya's first full-length book published by Ignota Books in 2019.

+ Leanne Betasamosake Simpson is a Michi Saagiig Nishnaabeg writer, scholar, and musician, and is a member of Alderville First Nation in Ontario, Canada. Her books include *A Short History of the Blockade* (2021), *Noopiming: The Cure for White Ladies* (2020), *This Accident of Being Lost* (2017), which won the MacEwan University Book of the Year, and *Islands of Decolonial Love* (2013). Her latest album, *The Theory of Ice*, is forthcoming in 2021. Simpson holds a PhD from the University of Manitoba and is faculty at the Dechinta Centre for Research.

+ Sin Wai Kin fka Victoria Sin is an artist using speculative fiction within performance, moving image, writing, and print to interrupt normative processes of desire, identification, and objectification. Drawing from close personal encounters of looking and wanting, their work presents heavily constructed fantasy narratives on the often unsettling experience of the physical within the social body.

+ Himali Singh Soin is a writer and artist based between London and Delhi. She uses metaphors from outer space and the natural environment to construct imaginary cosmologies of ecological loss and the loss of home, seeking shelter somewhere in the radicality of love. Her almanac (2017–ongoing) *we are opposite like that*, comprises missing paraphernalia from the polar archives, false philosophies, love letters, ekphrastic poems, and made-up maps.

+   Jenna Sutela works with words, sounds, and other living media, such as *Bacillus subtilis nattō* bacteria and the "many-headed" slime mold *Physarum polycephalum*. Her audio-visual pieces, sculptures, and performances seek to identify and react to precarious social and material moments, often in relation to technology. Sutela's work has been presented at museums and in art contexts including the Museum of Contemporary Art Tokyo, Moderna Museet, Stockholm, and the Serpentine Gallery in London. She was a Visiting Artist at The MIT Center for Art, Science & Technology (CAST) from 2019 to 2020.

+   Anna Lowenhaupt Tsing is Distinguished Professor of Anthropology at the University of California, Santa Cruz. Her books and projects include *Feral Atlas: The More-Than-Human Anthropocene* (2021), *Arts of Living on a Damaged Planet* (2017), *The Mushroom at the End of the World* (2015), *Friction: An Ethnography of Global Connection* (2005), and *In the Realm of the Diamond Queen* (1993).

Colophon

Das Neue Alphabet (The New Alphabet) is a publication series by HKW (Haus der Kulturen der Welt).

The series is part of the HKW project *Das Neue Alphabet* (2019–2022), supported by the Federal Government Commissioner for Culture and the Media due to a ruling of the German Bundestag.

Series Editors: Detlef Diederichsen, Anselm Franke, Katrin Klingan, Daniel Neugebauer, Bernd Scherer
Project Management: Philipp Albers
Managing Editor: Martin Hager
Copy-Editing: Mandi Gomez, Hannah Sarid de Mowbray
Design Concept: Olaf Nicolai with Malin Gewinner and Hannes Drißner

Band 6: *Carrier Bag Fiction*
Editors: Sarah Shin, Mathias Zeiske
Coordinators: Amélie Kroneis, Veronika Rau
Contributors: Sophia Al-Maria, Season Butler, Federico Campagna, Dorothee Elmiger, Anna Haifisch, Laurel Halo, Ursula K. Le Guin, Taylor Le Melle, Enis Maci, Leanne Betasamosake Simpson, Sin Wai Kin, Himali Singh Soin, Jenna Sutela, Nisha Ramayya, Anna Tsing
Translators: Amanda DeMarco, Megan Ewing
Graphic-Design: Malin Gewinner, Hannes Drißner, Markus Dreßen
Type-Setting: Hannah Witte
DNA-Lettering (Cover): Hannes Drißner
Fonts: FK Raster (Florian Karsten), Suisse BP Int'l (Ian Party) Lyon Text (Kai Bernau)
Image Editing: ScanColor Reprostudio GmbH, Leipzig
Printing and Binding: Gutenberg Beuys Feindruckerei GmbH, Langenhagen

Published by:
Spector Books
Harkortstr. 10
01407 Leipzig
www.spectorbooks.com

Image Credits

Pages 11, 15, 28, 61, 63, 69, 75 Laurel Halo. *World Without Heroes*,
2021. Find the EP on laurelhalo.bandcamp.com
Pages 18/19 Jenna Sutela. *nimiia cétiï*, 2018. Rendering: Leïth
Benkhedda; page 25 Jenna Sutela. *Bacillus subtilis nattō to z
via VAE*, 2018. Rendering: Johannes Schnatmann. The artist
thanks Memo Akten for collaboration in machine learning on
the *nimiia cétiï* project.
Pages 50/51, 53, 54, 56/57 Sin Wai Kin fka Victoria Sin,
A Dream of Wholeness in Parts, 2021, film still. Courtesy the
artist, Chi-Wen Gallery, Taipei and Soft Opening, London.
Pages 78, 79, 80 Sophia Al-Maria. *Little Oom*, 2021.
Pages 84, 87, 88 Anna Haifisch

The work on this publication was supported by the DAAD
Artists-in-Berlin Program.

Distribution:
Germany, Austria: GVA Gemeinsame Verlagsauslieferung
        Göttingen GmbH & Co. KG, www.gva-verlage.de
Switzerland: AVA Verlagsauslieferung AG, www.ava.ch
France, Belgium: Interart Paris, www.interart.fr
UK: Central Books Ltd, www.centralbooks.com
USA, Canada, Central and South America, Africa:
        ARTBOOK | D.A.P. www.artbook.com
Japan: twelvebooks, www.twelve-books.com
South Korea: The Book Society, www.thebooksociety.org
Australia, New Zealand: Perimeter Distribution,
        www.perimeterdistribution.com

Haus der Kulturen der Welt
John-Foster-Dulles-Allee 10
D-10557 Berlin
www.hkw.de

Haus der Kulturen der Welt

Haus der Kulturen der Welt is a business division of Kultur-
veranstaltungen des Bundes in Berlin GmbH (KBB).

Director: Bernd Scherer
Managing Director: Charlotte Sieben
Chairwoman of the Supervisory Board: Federal
        Government Commissioner for Culture and the Media
        Prof. Monika Grütters MdB

Haus der Kulturen der Welt is supported by

 Minister of State
for Culture and the Media

 Federal Foreign Office

First Edition
Printed in Germany
ISBN: 978-3-95905-463-8